EMMANUEL JOSEPH

From Code to Concrete, The Human Tales of Silicon Valley Titans and Real Estate Moguls

Copyright © 2025 by Emmanuel Joseph

All rights reserved. No part of this publication may be reproduced, stored or transmitted in any form or by any means, electronic, mechanical, photocopying, recording, scanning, or otherwise without written permission from the publisher. It is illegal to copy this book, post it to a website, or distribute it by any other means without permission.

First edition

This book was professionally typeset on Reedsy. Find out more at reedsy.com

Contents

1. Chapter 1: The Origins of Silicon Valley — 1
2. Chapter 2: From Startups to Titans — 3
3. Chapter 3: The Real Estate Boom — 5
4. Chapter 4: The Human Element — 7
5. Chapter 5: The Innovators — 9
6. Chapter 6: The Real Estate Visionaries — 11
7. Chapter 7: The Cultural Shift — 13
8. Chapter 8: Women in Silicon Valley — 15
9. Chapter 9: The Future of Silicon Valley — 18
10. Chapter 10: The Environmental Impact — 20
11. Chapter 11: Philanthropy and Giving Back — 22
12. Chapter 12: The Human Legacy — 25

1

Chapter 1: The Origins of Silicon Valley

Silicon Valley, the epicenter of technological innovation, didn't start with sleek gadgets or futuristic software. It began with the dreams of a few visionaries, who saw potential in silicon chips and coding languages. In the 1960s and 1970s, men like Gordon Moore and Robert Noyce laid the groundwork for what would become a technological revolution. Their stories are intertwined with the struggle for funding, the drive to innovate, and the relentless pursuit of perfection. These pioneers turned garages into laboratories and transformed their humble beginnings into empires.

The journey of these early visionaries wasn't just about technology; it was about the belief that they could change the world. Their relentless pursuit of innovation paved the way for the modern tech landscape. Moore and Noyce, among others, faced numerous obstacles, from limited resources to skepticism from established industries. Yet, their unwavering commitment to their vision set the stage for the tech boom that would follow. The culture of Silicon Valley, characterized by collaboration and a willingness to take risks, was born from their efforts.

As the foundation of Silicon Valley was being built, the region began to attract talent and investment. Universities like Stanford played a crucial role in nurturing this ecosystem, providing both intellectual capital and entrepreneurial spirit. The proximity to these academic institutions fostered a symbiotic relationship between education and industry. This connection would prove instrumental in the rapid growth and success of Silicon Valley. The blend of academia, industry, and venture capital created a unique environment that encouraged innovation and entrepreneurship.

The early days of Silicon Valley were marked by a sense of community and collaboration. Innovators worked together, sharing ideas and resources, driven by a common goal. This spirit of cooperation and mutual support became a defining characteristic of the region. The informal networks and partnerships that emerged played a pivotal role in the success of many early tech companies. This collaborative ethos continues to be a cornerstone of Silicon Valley's identity, driving its ongoing success and evolution.

In the midst of this technological revolution, the human stories often get overshadowed by the achievements. The personal journeys of these pioneers, their struggles, failures, and triumphs, are an integral part of the Silicon Valley narrative. Behind every technological breakthrough, there are countless hours of hard work, moments of doubt, and bursts of inspiration. These human tales remind us that at the heart of Silicon Valley's success are the people who dared to dream and persevere.

2

Chapter 2: From Startups to Titans

As Silicon Valley grew, so did its influence. The small startups that once struggled for survival began to morph into titans of the industry. Companies like Apple, Microsoft, and Google emerged from this fertile ground, each with its own unique origin story. These companies were not just businesses; they were movements. The people behind them—Steve Jobs, Bill Gates, and Larry Page—were not just entrepreneurs; they were visionaries. Their tales are filled with risks, failures, and extraordinary successes.

The rise of these tech giants was fueled by a combination of innovation, strategic vision, and sheer determination. Apple, for instance, started in a garage, with Steve Jobs and Steve Wozniak working tirelessly to bring their vision to life. Their journey from a small startup to a global powerhouse is a testament to the power of innovation and perseverance. Similarly, Bill Gates and Paul Allen's creation of Microsoft transformed the software industry, revolutionizing the way people interacted with computers. Their stories are a blend of brilliant ideas, calculated risks, and an unwavering belief in their mission.

Google's rise to prominence is another remarkable tale of Silicon Valley success. Founded by Larry Page and Sergey Brin while they were Ph.D. students at Stanford, Google began as a research project that aimed to improve internet search. Their innovative approach and commitment to providing accurate and relevant search results quickly set them apart from competitors. The company's rapid growth and expansion into various domains, from advertising to mobile operating systems, highlight the dynamic nature of Silicon Valley's tech landscape. Google's journey underscores the importance of adaptability and a willingness to explore new frontiers.

The culture of these tech titans played a significant role in their success. They fostered environments that encouraged creativity, collaboration, and calculated risk-taking. Open workspaces, flat organizational structures, and a focus on employee well-being became hallmarks of Silicon Valley companies. This emphasis on fostering a positive and innovative work culture attracted top talent from around the world, further fueling the growth of these tech giants. The stories of these companies and their leaders highlight the crucial role that company culture plays in driving innovation and success.

As these startups evolved into industry leaders, their impact extended beyond the tech sector. They influenced various aspects of society, from the way people communicate to how they access information. The innovations born in Silicon Valley have reshaped industries, created new markets, and transformed everyday life. The stories of these tech titans are a testament to the power of vision, innovation, and relentless pursuit of excellence. They serve as an inspiration for future generations of entrepreneurs and innovators, reminding us that great things can emerge from humble beginnings.

3

Chapter 3: The Real Estate Boom

With the rise of tech giants came the demand for space—both for living and working. Real estate in Silicon Valley became one of the most coveted and expensive in the world. This chapter explores the intersection of technology and real estate, highlighting the moguls who saw an opportunity in the growing demand. Figures like Donald Bren and the Irvine Company capitalized on this boom, transforming barren lands into bustling communities. The challenges they faced were immense, from regulatory hurdles to environmental concerns.

The transformation of Silicon Valley's landscape was driven by visionary real estate developers who recognized the potential for growth. Donald Bren, for example, played a significant role in shaping the region's real estate market. His strategic investments and development projects helped create vibrant communities that catered to the needs of the tech workforce. The Irvine Company, under Bren's leadership, developed master-planned communities that combined residential, commercial, and recreational spaces. These developments provided a blueprint for sustainable and integrated urban planning.

The rapid growth of the tech industry brought with it a surge in demand for office space and housing. Real estate developers responded by constructing state-of-the-art office buildings, residential complexes, and mixed-use developments. The influx of tech professionals and their families drove the demand for amenities such as schools, parks, and shopping centers. Developers like John Arrillaga and Charles Schwab played a crucial role in meeting this demand, creating iconic structures that became symbols of Silicon Valley's growth. Their efforts not only provided the necessary infrastructure but also contributed to the region's aesthetic appeal.

The real estate boom in Silicon Valley also brought challenges, particularly in terms of affordability and sustainability. The skyrocketing property prices made it difficult for many people, including essential workers, to afford housing. This led to concerns about gentrification and displacement of long-time residents. Real estate developers had to navigate these challenges while striving to create inclusive and diverse communities. Initiatives such as affordable housing projects and community engagement programs aimed to address these issues and promote social equity.

As Silicon Valley continued to expand, the focus shifted towards sustainable development practices. Real estate developers embraced green building technologies and environmentally friendly designs. The goal was to minimize the ecological footprint of new developments and promote energy efficiency. Projects incorporating renewable energy sources, water conservation measures, and green spaces became increasingly common. These efforts highlighted the importance of balancing technological progress with environmental stewardship, ensuring that Silicon Valley's growth was sustainable in the long run.

4

Chapter 4: The Human Element

Behind every code written and every building constructed, there are human stories. This chapter delves into the personal lives of Silicon Valley's tech geniuses and real estate moguls. It explores their motivations, their struggles, and their triumphs. From the long nights coding in isolation to the boardroom battles over billion-dollar deals, these individuals are more than their professional achievements. They are fathers, mothers, friends, and dreamers.

The human element of Silicon Valley is often overshadowed by the technological advancements and financial successes. However, the personal journeys of these individuals are filled with moments of vulnerability, resilience, and determination. Tech pioneers like Steve Jobs and Elon Musk faced numerous setbacks and challenges on their paths to success. Jobs' battle with cancer and Musk's struggles with depression are reminders that even the most successful individuals face personal hardships. Their ability to overcome these challenges and continue to innovate is a testament to their strength and perseverance.

The personal lives of real estate moguls also reveal the complexities of their journeys. Figures like Donald Bren and John Arrillaga had to navigate the intricacies of the real estate market while balancing their personal commitments. Bren, known for his philanthropy and commitment to education, faced criticism and legal battles throughout his career. Arrillaga, a former basketball player, brought his competitive spirit and teamwork ethos to the real estate industry. Their stories highlight the importance of resilience, adaptability, and a strong support system in achieving success.

Relationships and partnerships played a crucial role in the success of Silicon Valley's tech and real estate leaders. The collaboration between Steve Jobs and Steve Wozniak, for example, was instrumental in the creation of Apple. Similarly, the partnership between Larry Page and Sergey Brin led to the founding of Google. These partnerships were built on mutual respect, shared vision, and complementary skills. The ability to work together towards a common goal was a defining characteristic of many successful ventures in Silicon Valley.

The human element also extends to the broader community of Silicon Valley. The region's success is built on the contributions of countless individuals, from engineers and designers to educators and community leaders. The collaborative spirit and sense of community are integral to the culture of Silicon Valley. This chapter celebrates the diverse and dynamic individuals who have played a role in shaping the region. Their stories remind us that behind every innovation and development, there are people with dreams, passions, and aspirations.

5

Chapter 5: The Innovators

Innovation is the heartbeat of Silicon Valley. This chapter celebrates the unsung heroes—the engineers, designers, and developers who bring ideas to life. It explores the collaborative spirit that drives the tech community, where failure is seen as a stepping stone to success. Through interviews and anecdotes, we learn about the breakthroughs that have shaped our digital world. From the creation of the first microprocessor to the development of artificial intelligence, these stories highlight the ingenuity and persistence that define Silicon Valley.

The journey of an innovator in Silicon Valley is one of relentless pursuit of new ideas and solutions. Engineers and developers often work in teams, combining their expertise to tackle complex challenges. This collaborative environment fosters a culture of continuous learning and experimentation. Companies like Google and Facebook have become known for their innovative workspaces, designed to encourage creativity and interaction among employees. The stories of these innovators are filled with moments of inspiration and discovery, as well as setbacks and failures that ultimately lead to breakthroughs.

The process of innovation is not without its challenges. Silicon Valley's innovators face intense competition and pressure to deliver results. The rapid pace of technological advancement means that staying ahead of the curve requires constant adaptation and agility. Innovators must navigate the complexities of intellectual property, regulatory frameworks, and market dynamics. Despite these challenges, the drive to create something new and impactful keeps them going. The stories of these individuals highlight the resilience and determination required to succeed in the ever-evolving tech landscape.

The impact of innovation extends beyond the confines of Silicon Valley. The technologies and products developed by these innovators have transformed industries and reshaped the way we live and work. From smartphones and social media platforms to electric vehicles and renewable energy solutions, the influence of Silicon Valley's innovation is felt worldwide. This chapter explores the far-reaching effects of these technological advancements and the ways in which they have changed our daily lives. The stories of the innovators behind these breakthroughs provide a glimpse into the creative process and the vision that drives them.

The culture of innovation in Silicon Valley is characterized by a willingness to take risks and embrace failure as a learning opportunity. This mindset has led to the creation of numerous groundbreaking technologies and companies. The stories of successful startups like Airbnb, Uber, and Tesla are testaments to the power of innovation and the entrepreneurial spirit. These companies started with bold ideas and faced numerous challenges along the way, but their founders' perseverance and commitment to their vision ultimately led to success. The lessons learned from their journeys continue to inspire the next generation of innovators.

6

Chapter 6: The Real Estate Visionaries

In parallel to the tech revolution, real estate visionaries were reshaping the physical landscape. This chapter profiles the leaders who transformed Silicon Valley's skyline. Developers like John Arrillaga and Charles Schwab had a keen eye for potential and a knack for turning ideas into reality. They navigated complex financial landscapes, forged strategic partnerships, and built structures that became iconic symbols of Silicon Valley's growth. Their stories are a testament to the power of vision and determination in the face of adversity.

The real estate visionaries of Silicon Valley recognized the potential for growth and development in the region. They saw opportunities where others saw challenges and took bold steps to capitalize on them. John Arrillaga, for example, played a significant role in the development of commercial real estate in Silicon Valley. His projects included office parks, research facilities, and mixed-use developments that provided the infrastructure needed to support the burgeoning tech industry. Arrillaga's vision and strategic investments helped shape the landscape of Silicon Valley and create a vibrant business environment.

Charles Schwab, another prominent figure in Silicon Valley's real estate scene, brought his financial acumen and innovative approach to real estate development. Schwab's projects focused on creating sustainable and community-oriented developments that catered to the needs of both businesses and residents. His commitment to quality and attention to detail set new standards for real estate development in the region. Schwab's story is one of perseverance and adaptability, as he navigated the complexities of the real estate market and built a successful and enduring legacy.

The real estate visionaries of Silicon Valley faced numerous challenges in their pursuit of development. Regulatory hurdles, environmental concerns, and economic fluctuations were just a few of the obstacles they had to overcome. However, their ability to anticipate trends, build strategic partnerships, and innovate in their approach allowed them to succeed. The stories of these visionaries highlight the importance of resilience and adaptability in the face of adversity. Their contributions to the growth and development of Silicon Valley have left a lasting impact on the region.

The impact of real estate development in Silicon Valley extends beyond the physical structures. The developments created by visionaries like Arrillaga and Schwab have contributed to the region's economic growth, job creation, and community development. The mixed-use developments and master-planned communities they built have become vibrant hubs of activity, attracting businesses, residents, and visitors alike. The success of these developments has also inspired a new generation of real estate professionals who continue to push the boundaries of innovation in the industry.

The legacy of Silicon Valley's real estate visionaries is a testament to the power of vision and determination. Their stories serve as an inspiration for future generations of developers and entrepreneurs. The innovative approaches and bold decisions they made have shaped the region's landscape and contributed to its success. The lessons learned from their journeys continue to influence the real estate industry and provide valuable insights for those looking to make their mark in Silicon Valley.

7

Chapter 7: The Cultural Shift

The rise of Silicon Valley brought about significant cultural changes. This chapter examines the impact of tech and real estate development on the local communities. It discusses the challenges of gentrification, the shift in socio-economic dynamics, and the cultural blending that defines the region. Through the eyes of residents, workers, and community leaders, we gain insight into how Silicon Valley's evolution has shaped everyday life. The balance between progress and preservation is a recurring theme, highlighting the delicate interplay between growth and community.

The rapid growth of Silicon Valley has led to a cultural shift in the region. The influx of tech professionals and the development of real estate have transformed the social and economic fabric of the area. The once predominantly agricultural region has become a hub of innovation and opportunity. This transformation has brought about changes in lifestyle, work culture, and social dynamics. The stories of long-time residents and newcomers provide a glimpse into the evolving culture of Silicon Valley.

One of the significant challenges associated with Silicon Valley's growth is gentrification. The rising cost of living and housing prices have made it difficult for many long-time residents to afford to stay in the area. This has led to concerns about displacement and the loss of community identity. The experiences of residents facing these challenges highlight the need for inclusive and equitable development practices. Efforts to address these issues, such as affordable housing initiatives and community engagement programs, aim to create a more balanced and inclusive Silicon Valley.

The cultural shift in Silicon Valley is also characterized by the blending of diverse communities. The region attracts talent from around the world, creating a melting pot of cultures, ideas, and perspectives. This diversity has enriched the cultural landscape of Silicon Valley, fostering innovation and creativity. The stories of individuals from different backgrounds and their contributions to the tech and real estate sectors highlight the importance of diversity and inclusion in driving progress. The cultural exchange and collaboration between different communities have become a defining feature of Silicon Valley.

The impact of tech and real estate development on local communities is multifaceted. While the growth of Silicon Valley has brought economic prosperity and job opportunities, it has also posed challenges related to infrastructure, transportation, and environmental sustainability. Community leaders and advocates play a crucial role in addressing these challenges and ensuring that development benefits all residents. Their stories and efforts to create a more sustainable and inclusive Silicon Valley are a testament to the importance of community engagement and collaboration.

The balance between progress and preservation is a recurring theme in Silicon Valley's evolution. As the region continues to grow, there is a need to preserve its cultural heritage and natural environment. The efforts to protect historic landmarks, green spaces, and cultural institutions highlight the importance of maintaining a sense of identity and continuity. The stories of individuals and organizations working towards these goals underscore the significance of preserving the unique character of Silicon Valley while embracing innovation and progress.

8

Chapter 8: Women in Silicon Valley

While Silicon Valley has often been criticized for its gender imbalance, there are remarkable stories of women who have made their mark. This chapter shines a light on the female pioneers who broke barriers and shattered glass ceilings. From early trailblazers like Ada Lovelace to contemporary leaders like Sheryl Sandberg and Marissa Mayer, their journeys are inspiring. Their stories highlight the importance of diversity and inclusion in fostering innovation. Through their experiences, we learn about the challenges they faced and the triumphs they achieved.

The contributions of women to Silicon Valley's success are both significant and inspiring. Ada Lovelace, often regarded as the world's first computer programmer, laid the foundation for future generations of women in technology. Her pioneering work in the 19th century set the stage for the development of modern computing. Lovelace's story is a testament to the importance of vision and innovation, even in the face of societal constraints. Her legacy continues to inspire women in STEM fields and serves as a reminder of the potential for women to make groundbreaking contributions.

In contemporary Silicon Valley, women like Sheryl Sandberg and Marissa Mayer have risen to prominent leadership positions in major tech companies. Sandberg, as the COO of Facebook, has been a vocal advocate for gender equality and empowerment. Her book, "Lean In," has sparked important conversations about the challenges women face in the workplace and the importance of supporting female leaders. Mayer, as the former CEO of Yahoo, navigated the complexities of leading a major tech company while balancing personal and professional responsibilities. Their stories highlight the resilience, determination, and leadership qualities that women bring to the tech industry.

The journeys of these female pioneers are not without challenges. Women in Silicon Valley often face gender bias, discrimination, and a lack of representation in The journeys of these female pioneers are not without challenges. Women in Silicon Valley often face gender bias, discrimination, and a lack of representation in leadership positions. Despite these obstacles, they have made significant strides and continue to break barriers. Programs and initiatives aimed at promoting gender diversity and inclusion have played a crucial role in supporting women's careers in tech. Organizations like Girls Who Code and Women in Tech are empowering the next generation of female leaders and innovators, ensuring that their voices are heard and their contributions recognized.

The stories of women in Silicon Valley also highlight the importance of mentorship and support networks. Many female leaders have benefited from the guidance and encouragement of mentors who have helped them navigate their careers. These mentorship relationships provide valuable insights, advice, and opportunities for growth. The experiences of women like Susan Wojcicki, CEO of YouTube, and Ginni Rometty, former CEO of IBM, underscore the impact of mentorship in fostering success. Their journeys serve as an inspiration for aspiring female tech professionals, demonstrating that with the right support and determination, they can achieve their goals.

In addition to their professional achievements, many women in Silicon Valley are actively involved in philanthropic efforts and advocacy. Leaders like Melinda Gates and Laurene Powell Jobs are using their platforms and resources to address pressing social issues, from education and healthcare to gender equality and environmental sustainability. Their commitment to making a positive impact extends beyond the tech industry, highlighting the broader role that women can play in driving change. The stories of

CHAPTER 8: WOMEN IN SILICON VALLEY

these female philanthropists and advocates showcase the power of leveraging success for the greater good.

The progress made by women in Silicon Valley is a testament to their resilience, innovation, and leadership. Their contributions have shaped the tech industry and set the stage for future advancements. As more women enter the field and take on leadership roles, the landscape of Silicon Valley continues to evolve. This chapter celebrates the achievements of female pioneers and emphasizes the importance of diversity and inclusion in fostering innovation. The stories of these remarkable women inspire us to continue working towards a more equitable and inclusive future.

9

Chapter 9: The Future of Silicon Valley

As we look to the future, Silicon Valley continues to evolve. This chapter explores the emerging trends and technologies that will shape the next chapter of its story. From advancements in artificial intelligence to breakthroughs in biotechnology, the future is filled with possibilities. The leaders of tomorrow are already making their mark, and their stories are just beginning. This chapter offers a glimpse into the exciting developments on the horizon and the new frontiers that Silicon Valley will conquer.

The rapid pace of technological innovation shows no signs of slowing down. Artificial intelligence, in particular, is poised to revolutionize various industries, from healthcare and finance to transportation and entertainment. Startups and established companies alike are exploring the potential of AI to solve complex problems and improve efficiency. The stories of AI pioneers, such as Demis Hassabis of DeepMind and Fei-Fei Li of Stanford University, highlight the transformative power of this technology. Their work is paving the way for a future where AI is seamlessly integrated into our daily lives, enhancing our capabilities and opening new possibilities.

Biotechnology is another field with immense potential for growth and innovation. Silicon Valley has become a hub for biotech startups and research institutions focused on developing cutting-edge medical treatments and therapies. Advances in gene editing, personalized medicine, and regenerative

CHAPTER 9: THE FUTURE OF SILICON VALLEY

medicine are promising to revolutionize healthcare and improve patient outcomes. The stories of biotech entrepreneurs and researchers, such as Jennifer Doudna and Emmanuelle Charpentier, who co-discovered CRISPR-Cas9, illustrate the groundbreaking work being done in this field. Their contributions are reshaping the landscape of medicine and offering hope for cures to previously untreatable diseases.

The future of Silicon Valley is also being shaped by a growing emphasis on sustainability and environmental responsibility. As the region continues to expand, there is an increasing focus on developing eco-friendly technologies and practices. Startups and established companies are investing in renewable energy, sustainable agriculture, and green building practices. The stories of environmental innovators, such as Elon Musk with Tesla and SolarCity, highlight the importance of creating a more sustainable future. Their work is driving the adoption of clean technologies and setting new standards for environmental stewardship.

The next generation of Silicon Valley leaders is characterized by a commitment to diversity and inclusion. Efforts to promote gender, racial, and cultural diversity are gaining momentum, with companies recognizing the value of diverse perspectives in driving innovation. Initiatives such as diversity hiring programs, mentorship schemes, and inclusive workplace policies are helping to create a more equitable tech industry. The stories of emerging leaders who champion diversity, such as Arlan Hamilton of Backstage Capital and Reshma Saujani of Girls Who Code, underscore the importance of creating an inclusive environment where everyone can thrive.

As Silicon Valley looks to the future, its success will continue to be driven by the spirit of innovation, collaboration, and resilience. The region's ability to adapt to changing circumstances and embrace new technologies will ensure its continued growth and relevance. The stories of the visionaries, entrepreneurs, and innovators who are shaping the future of Silicon Valley provide a glimpse into the exciting developments on the horizon. This chapter celebrates their contributions and offers a hopeful vision for the next chapter of Silicon Valley's story.

10

Chapter 10: The Environmental Impact

With great growth comes great responsibility. This chapter addresses the environmental challenges that accompany Silicon Valley's expansion. It discusses the efforts being made to create sustainable practices and reduce the ecological footprint. From green buildings to renewable energy initiatives, Silicon Valley's innovators are also environmental stewards. Their stories underscore the importance of balancing technological progress with environmental preservation.

The rapid growth of Silicon Valley has had a significant impact on the environment. The increased demand for office space, housing, and infrastructure has led to concerns about land use, resource consumption, and pollution. However, many tech companies and real estate developers are taking proactive steps to address these challenges. Initiatives such as LEED-certified buildings, energy-efficient designs, and waste reduction programs are becoming standard practices in the region. The stories of companies like Google and Apple, which have invested in renewable energy and sustainable campus designs, highlight the importance of integrating environmental considerations into business operations.

Green building practices are at the forefront of Silicon Valley's efforts to create a more sustainable future. Developers are incorporating features such as solar panels, green roofs, and energy-efficient HVAC systems into their projects. These innovations not only reduce the environmental

CHAPTER 10: THE ENVIRONMENTAL IMPACT

impact of buildings but also create healthier and more productive work environments. The experiences of developers like John Arrillaga, who have embraced sustainable design principles, demonstrate the benefits of prioritizing environmental stewardship in real estate development. Their projects serve as models for sustainable urban planning and development.

Renewable energy initiatives are another key component of Silicon Valley's sustainability efforts. Many tech companies are investing in solar, wind, and other renewable energy sources to power their operations. Tesla's development of solar energy solutions and battery storage systems is a prime example of how innovation can drive the transition to clean energy. The stories of renewable energy pioneers like Elon Musk and Lyndon Rive highlight the importance of creating a resilient and sustainable energy infrastructure. Their work is not only reducing carbon emissions but also inspiring other companies to follow suit.

Efforts to reduce the ecological footprint of Silicon Valley extend beyond individual companies and developments. Regional initiatives and collaborations are playing a crucial role in addressing environmental challenges. The Silicon Valley Leadership Group, for example, brings together business leaders, policymakers, and community organizations to promote sustainable practices and policies. Their efforts to improve public transportation, reduce water usage, and promote clean energy adoption are helping to create a more sustainable and resilient region. The stories of these collaborative initiatives underscore the importance of collective action in addressing environmental issues.

The commitment to environmental sustainability in Silicon Valley is a testament to the region's forward-thinking and innovative spirit. By prioritizing sustainable practices and technologies, Silicon Valley is setting an example for other regions to follow. The stories of environmental stewards and innovators highlight the importance of balancing growth with environmental preservation. As the region continues to evolve, its commitment to sustainability will play a crucial role in ensuring a thriving and resilient future for Silicon Valley and beyond.

11

Chapter 11: Philanthropy and Giving Back

Many of Silicon Valley's most successful individuals have turned their attention to philanthropy. This chapter explores the charitable endeavors of tech titans and real estate moguls. Figures like Bill Gates and Elon Musk have used their wealth to address global challenges, from healthcare to education. Their stories highlight the power of giving back and the impact of using resources for the greater good. Through their philanthropy, they are shaping a better future for all.

Philanthropy has become an integral part of Silicon Valley's culture. Many tech leaders and entrepreneurs are committed to using their wealth and influence to make a positive impact on society. Bill Gates, co-founder of Microsoft, is one of the most prominent examples of this commitment. Through the Bill and Melinda Gates Foundation, Gates has focused on addressing global health issues, improving education, and reducing poverty. His philanthropic efforts have led to significant advancements in areas such as vaccine development, disease eradication, and access to education. Gates' story is a powerful example of how philanthropy can drive meaningful change and improve lives.

Elon Musk, known for his innovative ventures in space exploration and renewable energy, is also dedicated to philanthropic efforts. Musk's

CHAPTER 11: PHILANTHROPY AND GIVING BACK

philanthropic initiatives include contributions to renewable energy projects, disaster relief efforts, and education programs. His foundation, the Musk Foundation, focuses on promoting sustainable energy, advancing space exploration, and supporting research and education in various fields. Musk's commitment to addressing global challenges through philanthropy reflects his broader vision of creating a better and more sustainable future for humanity.

The real estate moguls of Silicon Valley are also making significant contributions to philanthropy. Figures like Donald Bren and John Arrillaga have used their wealth to support education, healthcare, and community development initiatives. Bren, for example, has donated millions to educational institutions, medical research, and environmental conservation projects. Arrillaga's philanthropic efforts include substantial contributions to Stanford University, supporting scholarships, research, and infrastructure development. Their stories highlight the

Chapter 11: Philanthropy and Giving Back (continued) Their stories highlight the significant impact that real estate moguls can have on their communities. By supporting various philanthropic initiatives, these leaders are helping to address critical issues such as education, healthcare, and social services. Their contributions are making a tangible difference in the lives of individuals and families, creating a ripple effect that extends beyond Silicon Valley.

Philanthropic efforts in Silicon Valley are not limited to financial contributions. Many tech and real estate leaders are also dedicating their time and expertise to support nonprofit organizations and community initiatives. They serve on boards, mentor aspiring entrepreneurs, and volunteer their skills to help drive positive change. The stories of these individuals highlight the importance of giving back in ways that go beyond monetary donations. Their commitment to making a difference through hands-on involvement and leadership is a powerful example of how philanthropy can take many forms.

The collaborative nature of Silicon Valley's philanthropic community is another key factor in its success. Tech companies, foundations, and nonprofit organizations often work together to address complex social issues. This collaborative approach allows for the pooling of resources, knowledge, and expertise, leading to more effective and sustainable solutions. Initiatives like the Chan Zuckerberg Initiative, founded by Mark Zuckerberg and Priscilla Chan, exemplify this spirit of collaboration. Their focus on leveraging technology and data to drive social change highlights the potential for innovative approaches to philanthropy.

The impact of Silicon Valley's philanthropic efforts extends beyond the local community. Many tech and real estate leaders are involved in global initiatives aimed at addressing pressing issues such as climate change, poverty, and access to education. Their contributions are helping to create a more just and equitable world. The stories of these global efforts highlight the interconnectedness of our world and the importance of addressing challenges on a global scale. The commitment of Silicon Valley's leaders to making a positive impact reflects the broader values of innovation and social responsibility that define the region.

Philanthropy in Silicon Valley is a testament to the power of using success for the greater good. The stories of tech titans and real estate moguls who have dedicated their resources to philanthropic endeavors highlight the potential for positive change. Their contributions are shaping a better future for all, demonstrating that the true measure of success lies not only in financial achievements but also in the impact one can have on the world. The legacy of philanthropy in Silicon Valley serves as an inspiration for future generations to continue the tradition of giving back.

12

Chapter 12: The Human Legacy

In the end, the true legacy of Silicon Valley lies not in its technology or skyscrapers, but in its people. This chapter reflects on the human stories that define the region. It celebrates the dreamers, the doers, and the believers who have made Silicon Valley what it is today. Their tales are a reminder that behind every innovation and every building, there is a human story. As we look to the future, it is these stories that will continue to inspire and drive us forward.

The human legacy of Silicon Valley is built on the dreams and aspirations of countless individuals. From the early pioneers who laid the foundation for the tech revolution to the innovators and entrepreneurs who continue to push the boundaries of possibility, their stories are a testament to the power of vision and determination. The personal journeys of these individuals are filled with moments of inspiration, resilience, and triumph. Their experiences remind us that behind every technological advancement and development, there are people who dared to dream big and work tirelessly to achieve their goals.

The collaborative spirit and sense of community that define Silicon Valley are central to its human legacy. The region's success is built on the contributions of diverse and dynamic individuals who come together to share ideas, knowledge, and resources. The informal networks, partnerships, and mentorship relationships that have emerged in Silicon Valley have played a crucial role in fostering innovation and growth. The stories of these collaborations highlight the importance of working together towards a common goal and the power of collective effort.

The human legacy of Silicon Valley also includes the impact of its leaders on the broader community. Many tech and real estate leaders have used their success to drive positive change and address pressing social issues. Their philanthropic efforts, advocacy work, and commitment to social responsibility have created a ripple effect that extends beyond the region. The stories of these leaders highlight the importance of giving back and using one's influence for the greater good. Their contributions are shaping a better future for all and leaving a lasting legacy of compassion and service.

The future of Silicon Valley will continue to be shaped by the human stories that define it. The next generation of innovators, entrepreneurs, and leaders will build on the foundation laid by their predecessors. Their journeys will be marked by new challenges, opportunities, and achievements. The human legacy of Silicon Valley is a living, evolving narrative that reflects the spirit of innovation, resilience, and collaboration that defines the region. As we look to the future, it is these stories that will continue to inspire and drive us forward.

In conclusion, the true legacy of Silicon Valley lies in the people who have made it what it is today. Their stories of vision, determination, and collaboration are a testament to the power of human potential. As we celebrate the achievements of Silicon Valley, we must also honor the individuals whose dreams and efforts have shaped its success. Their legacy is a reminder that behind every innovation and development, there is a human story that continues to inspire and drive us forward.

Book Description: From Code to Concrete: The Human Tales of Silicon Valley Titans and Real Estate Moguls

Step into the world where technology meets real estate, and innovation shapes the landscape. "From Code to Concrete: The Human Tales of Silicon Valley Titans and Real Estate Moguls" takes you on a captivating journey through the heart of Silicon Valley.

This book unravels the stories behind the tech giants and real estate

CHAPTER 12: THE HUMAN LEGACY

visionaries who transformed a sleepy California region into a global hub of innovation and prosperity. From the humble beginnings of legendary startups to the rise of towering skyscrapers, the tales of these pioneers are interwoven with moments of triumph, struggle, and unwavering determination.

Discover the personal journeys of iconic figures like Steve Jobs, Bill Gates, and Larry Page, whose vision and drive created the tech empires that shape our digital world. Dive into the world of real estate moguls like Donald Bren and John Arrillaga, who saw potential in the growing demand for space and turned barren lands into thriving communities.

Explore the human element behind every breakthrough and building, where passion meets perseverance, and collaboration fosters creativity. Learn about the cultural shifts, the environmental impact, and the philanthropic efforts that define Silicon Valley's legacy.

"From Code to Concrete" is not just a chronicle of technological advancements and architectural marvels; it's a celebration of the people who dared to dream big and make their mark on the world. Their stories remind us that behind every innovation, there is a human tale of vision, determination, and resilience.

Join us as we delve into the heart of Silicon Valley, where code and concrete come together to shape the future. This book is a tribute to the dreamers, doers, and believers who continue to inspire and drive us forward.

www.ingramcontent.com/pod-product-compliance
Lightning Source LLC
LaVergne TN
LVHW020741090526
838202LV00057BA/6173